Scotland

Scotland

Clive Hardy

Waterton Press Limited

First published in the United Kingdom in 1998 by
Frith Publishing an imprint of Waterton Press Limited
Reprinted in 1999

British Library Cataloguing in Publication Data

Clive Hardy
Scotland

ISBN 1-84125-073-2

Reproductions of all the photographs in this book are
available as framed or mounted prints. For more
information please contact The Francis Frith Collection
at the address below quoting the title of this book and
the page number and photograph number or title.

The Francis Frith Collection,
'Friths Barn', Teffont, Salisbury, Wiltshire, SP3 5QP
Tel: 01722 716376
E mail: bookprints@francisfrith.com
Web pages: www.francisfrith.com

Typeset in Bembo Semi Bold

Printed and bound in Great Britain by
WBC Limited, Bridgend, Glamorgan.

Contents

Francis Frith 1822–1898

Introduction

Francis Frith: A Victorian Pioneer

Francis Frith, the founder of the world famous photographic archive was a complex and multitudinous man. A devout Quaker and a highly successful and respected Victorian businessman he was also a flamboyant character.

By 1855 Frith had already established a wholesale grocery business in Liverpool and sold it for the astonishing sum of £200,000, equivalent of over £15,000,000 today. Now a multi-millionaire he was able to indulge in his irresistible desire to travel. As a child he had pored over books penned by early explorers, and his imagination had been stirred by family holidays to the sublime mountain regions of Wales and Scotland. "What a land of spirit-stirring and enriching scenes and places!" he had written. He was to return to these scenes of grandeur in later years to "recapture the thousands of vivid and tender memories", but with a very different purpose. Now in his thirties, and captivated by the new science of photography, Frith set out on a series of pioneering journeys to the Middle East, that occupied him from 1856 until 1860.

He took with him a specially-designed wicker carriage which acted as camera, dark-room and sleeping chamber. These far-flung journeys were full of intrigue and adventure. In his life story, written when he was sixty-three, Frith tells of being held captive by bandits, and fighting "an awful midnight battle to the very point of exhaustion and surrender with a deadly pack of hungry, wild dogs". He bargained for several weeks with a "mysterious priest" over a beautiful seven-volume illuminated Koran, which is now in the British Museum. Wearing full arab costume, Frith arrived at Akaba by camel seventy years before Lawrence of Arabia, where he encountered "desert princes and rival sheikhs, blazing with jewel-hilted swords".

During these extraordinary adventures he was assiduously exploring the desert regions of the Nile and recording the antiquities and people with his camera, Frith was the first photographer ever to travel beyond the sixth cataract. Africa, we must remember, was still the "Dark Continent", and Stanley and Livingstone's famous meeting was a decade into the future. The conditions for picture taking confound belief. He laboured for hours on end in his dark-room in the sweltering heat, while the volatile collodion chemicals fizzed dangerously in their trays. Often he was forced to work in tombs and caves where conditions were cooler.

Back in London he exhibited his photographs and was "rapturously cheered" by the Royal Society. His reputation as a photographer was made overnight. His photographs were issued in albums by James S. Virtue and William MacKenzie, and published simultaneously in London and New York. An eminent historian has likened their impact on the population of the time to that on our own generation of the first photographs taken on the surface of the moon.

Characteristically, Frith spotted the potential to create a new business as a specialist publisher of photographs. In 1860 he married Mary Ann Rosling and set out to photograph every city, town and village in Britain. For the next thirty years Frith travelled the country by train and by pony and trap, producing photographs that were keenly bought by the millions of Victorians who, because of the burgeoning rail network, were beginning to enjoy holidays and day trips to Britain's seaside resorts and beauty spots.

To meet the demand he gathered together a team of up to twelve photographers, and also published the work of independent artist-photographers of the reputation of Roger Fenton and Francis Bedford. Together with clerks and photographic printers he employed a substantial staff at his Reigate studios. To gain an understanding of the scale of Frith's business one only has to look at the catalogue issued by Frith & Co. in 1886. It runs to some 670 pages listing not only many thousands of views of the British Isles but also photographs of most major European countries, and China, Japan, the USA and Canada. By 1890 Frith had created the greatest specialist photographic publishing company in the world.

He died in 1898 at his villa in Cannes, his great project still growing. His sons, Eustace and Cyril, took over the task, and Frith & Co. continued in business for another seventy years, until by 1970 the archive contained over a third of a million pictures of 7,000 cities, towns and villages.

The photographic record he has left to us stands as a living monument to a remarkable and very special man.

Frith's dhow in Egypt *c.*1857

CHAPTER 1
DUMFRIES & GALLOWAY

⸙ GRETNA ⸙

Gretna stands on the Scottish/English border and for this reason it became popular for runaway marriages of English couples following the passage of Lord Hardwicke's act in 1754. The act abolished irregular marriages in England but not Scotland.

⸙ MOFFAT ⸙

At the beginning of the twentieth century, Moffat attracted tourists wishing to sample the delights of the nearby sulphureous-saline wells. During the season the towns population of just more than 2,000 would more than double.

⸙ DUMFRIES ⸙

The River Nith divides Dumfries from Maxwelltown. Dumfries itself became a royal burgh in the twelfth century, but the two towns were not officially amalgamated until 1929. Robert Burns came to the town in 1791 and lived with his wife and family in a house in Millhole Brae. Burns died in 1796 at the age of 36 and is buried in St Michael's Church.

SARK BRIDGE, GRETNA, *c.*1955.   G163014

Once across the bridge runaways from England could be married very quickly in accordance with eighteenth century Scots law, neither banns nor a licence being necessary.

THE BLACKSMITH'S SHOP, GRETNA, *c.*1955 G163009

From 1826 this shop became the most popular place in Gretna for declaratory marriages. After 1856, a residence north of the border of not less than three weeks was required before a marriage could take place.

THE INTERIOR OF THE SMITHY, GRETNA, *c.*1955. G163008

Marriages also took place at Gretna Hall, Toll Inn and the Sark Toll Bar.

GRETNA HALL c.1955.

The hall was built in 1710. Hall records show that between 1825 and 1855 some 1,134 runaway marriages were performed in Gretna.

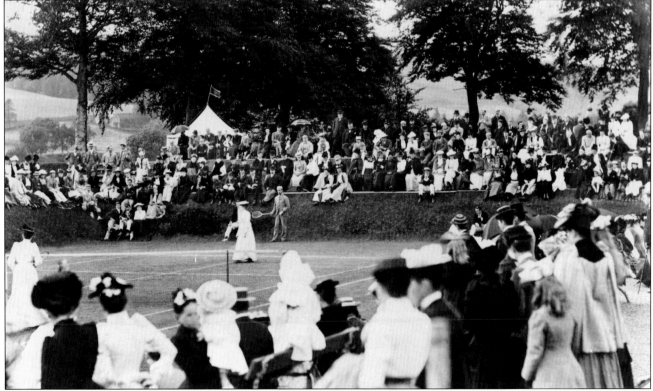

A TENNIS TOURNAMENT ATTRACTS THE CROWDS, MOFFAT, 1892.

The picture dates from 1892 and it was around this time that tennis became something of an event with most spa towns starting to hold annual tournaments.

MOFFAT HIGH STREET, 1890.   M113002

At this time Moffat was one of Scotland's chief inland resorts, boasting several hotels, a hydropathic establishment and private boarding houses.

GREYFRIARS CHURCH, DUMFRIES, c.1890.   D78002

It was here, in February 1306, that Robert Bruce killed John Comyn the Red. Five weeks later, Bruce was crowned King of Scotland and Edward I of England mobilized his northern levies.

CHAPTER 2
STRATHCLYDE

⬤ BOTHWELL ⬤

Three hundred years ago, Bothwell was a strategically important village, its bridge being the only one over the Clyde apart from Glasgow Bridge. In 1679, the Duke of Monmouth defeated the Covenanters at the Battle of Bothwell Brig.

⬤ GLASGOW ⬤

The Act of Union that joined Scotland with England established Glasgow's potential as a port and industrial centre. Glasgow was ideally situated to take advantage of the trade with the American colonies, and became the focus of the import and re-export of tobacco. American requirements for manufactured goods, such as textiles, transformed Scotland's linen industry to such an extent that by 1778 there were 4,000 handlooms in Glasgow alone. After the American War of Independence, the price of flax rocketed and cotton was looked upon as a viable alternative. By 1787, no less than nineteen cotton mills were at work, rising to more than 200 within a few decades.

In the 1750s, English iron founders discovered that it was cheaper to ship ore to Scotland for smelting due to the availability of cheap charcoal. However, it was the discovery in the early 1800s of a local source of top quality ironstone that gave the industry a much needed boost. By 1847, Scotland was producing 25 per cent of Britain's iron.

Glasgow was always a go-ahead sort of place. During the late seventeenth century a number of businesses were established including a soap works using whale blubber (1673), a sugar refinery (1675), a rope-works (1696) and a glass-works in 1700. There were also several candle factories and a number of coal-pits.

It was the advent of steam-power that saw the development of Glasgow's two greatest industries - shipbuilding and railway locomotives. The shipyards included Lobnitz & Co., W Simons & Co., John Brown & Co. Clydebank, A & J Inglis Ltd and D & W Henderson & Co. Railway locomotives were manufactured by the North British Locomotive Co., an amalgamation of three companies employing 7,000 workers. In total, the NBL built about 20,000 railway locomotives for customers world wide.

⬤ PAISLEY ⬤

By 1900, Paisley was an overcrowded, smoky, industrial town with a population approaching 80,000. Although spinning and weaving were the main industries there were also several shipyards along the banks of the River Cart. The longest lived was Fleming & Ferguson which specialised in building dredgers, hoppers and lighters. There was also the Thistle shipyard of Bow-McLachlan which had a reputation for building tugboats. The Thistle yard closed in the 1930s but was reopened during the Second World War for the construction of landing craft.

⁀ GREENOCK ⁀

It was in the seventeenth century that Greenock developed as a port, providing a packet service to and from Ireland. During the early years of the eighteenth century, facilities were improved with the construction of a harbour and quays. By 1760, the first shipyards at Greenock were open and in 1786 a graving dock was completed. One of the most famous yards was that of John Scott which built the first steamer to trade between Glasgow and Liverpool. The East India Harbour was completed in 1806-07, the Victoria Dock opened during the 1850s and the Albert Dock followed a decade or so later. A new graving dock was completed in the early 1870s and work on the James Watt Dock began in 1881.

⁀ GOUROCK ⁀

Once a few buildings huddled around a castle. It was from Gourock in 1494 that the energetic James IV sailed on his expedition to the Western Isles. Gourock was among the towns where witch hunts took place during the seventeenth century. One of the unfortunates who was burnt at the stake was a teenager by the name of Mary Lamont. The girl confessed, probably under torture, that she intended to throw Granny Kempock's Stone, (a pre-historic monolith of grey schist standing 6 ft high) into the sea so that ships might be wrecked upon it.

⁀ CLYDEBANK ⁀

Situated on the Clyde, opposite the mouth of the River Cart, Clydebank was little more than farmland until 1871-72, when J & G Thomson began the construction of a shipyard. At first there were no houses for the yard's workers; they were ferried to and from Glasgow by steamer. Clydebank with its six building berths, went into production in 1872 with three steamers for Thomas Skinner of Glasgow. A town eventually grew up on land behind the shipyard, the choice of name for it being a toss-up between Kilbowie and Clydebank. Clydebank was chosen, after the shipyard. In 1899, the yard was taken over by John Brown & Co of Sheffield.

⁀ ROTHESAY ⁀

The first effective spinning mill in the west of Scotland was built at Rothesay. Between 1787 and 1834, the number of cotton mills in Scotland rocketed from just 19 to 134. During the American Civil War the naval blockade by the North on Confederate ports caused American imports of cotton to fall from 8,600 tons in 1861, to 500 tons in 1862 and 350 tons in 1864. This in turn caused severe distress and hardship amongst British mill workers.

⁀ GREAT CUMBRAE ISLAND ⁀

Great Cumbrae Island in the Firth of Clyde is only about 10 miles in circumference . It is linked to the mainland by scheduled ferry services. Local industry once comprised fishing, weaving on handlooms and there was also a quarry.

⁀ GREAT CUMBRAE ISLAND ⁀

Great Cumbrae Island in the Firth of Clyde is only about 10 miles in circumference . It is linked to the mainland by scheduled ferry services. Local industry once comprised fishing, weaving on handlooms and there was also a quarry.

HELENSBURGH

Sir James Colquhoun of Luss developed Helensburgh in the late eighteenth century as a residential district for those who could afford not to have to live any nearer to Glasgow than was absolutely necessary. The coming of the railways put Helensburgh into the Glasgow commuter belt, whilst its steamer connections helped it to develop as a holiday centre. On the road to Loch Lomond is the entrance to Glen Fruin where, in 1603, clansmen loyal to Alastair MacGregor of Glenstrae clashed with, or rather massacred, 200 members of the Colquhoun clan. The MacGregors had been outlawed for relieving the Colquhouns of a few head of livestock, namely 300 beasts, 100 horses, 400 goats and 400 sheep. The MacGregors were hunted down, the clan proscribed for 173 years.

LOCH LOMOND

Loch Lomond became a popular destination for day trippers from around Clydeside especially after the opening of the Dumbarton & Balloch Joint Railway. The loch itself was served by the steamers of the Lochlomond Steam Boat Company, whose first ship, the *Prince of Wales* was built at Port Glasgow in 1858.

DUNOON

Until the early nineteenth century, Dunoon was nothing more than a small village clustered around a castle. The popularity of the Clyde excursion steamers changed all that and, within a short space of time, Dunoon developed into a holiday resort, the largest and best known on the Cowal.

LARGS

The bustling holiday town of Largs has long been famous as the site of a great battle in 1263 in which 16,000 Norwegians and 5,000 Scots were killed. There was certainly a battle and if there were any casualties they were light. Haakon of Norway's fleet had entered the Firth of Clyde when a storm drove 10 supply ships onto the beach at Largs. The Norweigian crews and the Scots fired a few arrows at each other but stopped when night fell. The following morning, Haakon himself landed on the beach with reinforcements, but instead of facing just a few locals, he found Alexander III's army. There was no pitched battle, only a couple of poorly co-ordinated horse charge along the beach. The Scots then withdrew and the Norwegians sailed away. The Battle of Largs was important because it led to the Treaty of Perth, under which Man and the Western Isles were purchased by the Scottish crown for 4,000 marks and an annual rent of 100 marks.

IRVINE

A royal burgh and port, Irvine was, by the 1920s, a town of 7,000 inhabitants. Many of these were employed in ironworking, chemical manufacturing and coal-mining, or in Nobel's dynamite works at Ardeer.

AYR

Famous as the birthplace of John Macadam in 1756 and Robert Burns in 1759, Ayr was founded under a charter granted by William the Lion. Little survives of the old town, although parts of the former Greyfriars church of St John, where Robert the Bruce held Parliament in 1315, are thought to date back to its beginnings.

BOTHWELL CASTLE, 1897. 39867

Dating back to the thirteenth century, this is one of the most impressive ruined fortresses in Scotland, the Douglas Tower took 36 years to build and is thought to be the work of French masons because it resembles a similar structure at Coucy in France.

ARGYLE STREET, GLASGOW, 1897. 39765

In late Victorian Glasgow, Argyle Street, Buchanan Street, Union Street and Sauchihall Street were considered the places for shopping.

BUCHANAN STREET, GLASGOW, 1897.   39767
This was one of the busiest thoroughfares in the city. At one end was the Caledonian Railway station where trains could be caught for Oban, Perth and the north; at the other was St Enoch Station. Buchanan Street was a great place to eat out with several top restaurants including Queen's at number 70 and Ferguson & Forrester at number 36.

A CONVOY OF HORSE-TRAMS TRUNDLE ALONG RENFIELD STREET, GLASGOW, 1897.   39769
Within a year, electric street trams would be running and the horse-trams phased out. Glasgow was the last city in the UK to abandon its tramway system. The Leeds system closed in 1959, Sheffield in 1960 and Glasgow in 1962.

GEORGE SQUARE, GLASGOW, 1897.
In the centre of the square is the 80 ft column surmounted by a statue of Sir Walter Scott. Other statues include those of Queen Victoria and Prince Albert, William Pitt, Sir Robert Peel, Robert Burns, Dr Livingstone, James Watt and Sir John Moore.

ST VINCENT'S PLACE LOOKING TOWARDS GEORGE SQUARE.   39764
St Vincent's Place was right in the commercial heart of the city with the National Bank, Royal Exchange, Stock Exchange, and Athenaeum club all nearby.

SAUCHIHALL STREET, 1897.   39763
Joining the east and west quarters of the city, this was where you could buy quality confectionery from *Assafrey* dine out at the *Hippodrome,* attend an exhibition at the Institute of Fine Arts, or stay at a temperance hotel.

THE GRAND HOTEL, GLASGOW, 1897.   39768
The Grand Hotel at the west end of Charing Cross had rooms from 3s 6d a night with dinner costing 5s.
The two most expensive hotels were the Central and the Windsor where rooms started at 4s 6d a night.
Most charged around 5s for dinner, although the Victoria in West George Street charged just 3s 6d.

GLASGOW CATHEDRAL AND NECROPOLIS, 1890.   G11001
The Cathedral stands on the site of an earlier building destroyed by fire in 1192. The choir and tower
date from the thirteenth century, the spire was added about two centuries later. The building is 320 ft
long, 70 ft wide and 90 ft high. The tower is 220 ft high. Behind the cathedral is the Necropolis
containing a number of substantial monuments to the great and the good as well as to those who had
enough money.

THE BOTANIC GARDENS OFF GREAT WESTERN ROAD, 1897. 39795
Many rare orchids, tree ferns and other plants grow here including bananas. The Kibble Palace is the largest glasshouse in Britain.

KELVINGROVE PARK, 1897. 39757
The central feature here is the Stewart memorial fountain. The park was chosen as the site for a museum and art gallery, which opened in 1901. For decades, the art gallery contained the finest municipal collection of Dutch, French and Scottish schools in Britain.

PAISLEY HIGH STREET, 1900.   45993

The rain appears to have stopped for the moment in this picture. Note the different styles of street lights. There are at least three on the right-hand side and on the left, the remains of gaslights are very much in evidence.

DUNN SQUARE, 1901.   47397

Paisley was the last stronghold of the highly skilled craft of fine handloom weaving, and as late as 1834 there were few if any power looms in the town. The Paisley weavers were specialists, producing goods for a luxury market. The end came not so much from power looms, but from printed imitations.

DUNN SQUARE, PAISLEY, 1897.

In 1906, Paisley was described as a 'smoke-begrimed industrial town on the Cart with 79,355 inhabitants and large thread (Coats & Clark), shawl and corn-flour (Brown & Poulson) factories.'

GRAHAM STREET, BARRHEAD, 1918.

By this time, calico-printing was losing its position as the town's main industry. the production of porcelain sanitary ware was taking over.

KILBARCHAN, 1884. K108001

In the mid eighteenth century, the town was noted for weaving, there being more than 1,000 handlooms in operation in the area. On the steeple of the church is a statue of Habbie Simpson, a well-known piper of the late sixteenth century.

UNION STREET, GREENOCK, 1899. 43405

Greenock was the birthplace, in 1736, of James Watt, who was born in a house on Dalrymple Street. The Watt Library and Institution was later built on Union Street.

THE VIEW FROM WHINHILL, 1899.
The smoking chimneypots of Greenock can be seen and the entrance to Gare Loch across the Firth of Clyde.

43400

GREENOCK HARBOUR, 1904. 52632

During the late seventeenth century, Greenock's herring trade with France and the Baltic required a fleet of more than 300 boats. The town motto was 'Let herring swim that trade maintain.' The herring went elsewhere and the trade declined.

AN EXCURSION STEAMER MANOEUVRES ALONGSIDE PRINCES PIER, GREENOCK, 1904. 52634

Owned by the Glasgow & South Western Railway, the pier was rebuilt and extended during 1892-94 and more than £20,000 was spent by the company on alterations to the pier railway station. The new buildings featured four Italianate towers constructed of red Ruabon brick.

A VIEW OVER THE ROOFTOPS FROM TOWER HILL, GOUROCK, 1900.   45965

The steamer crossing West Bay is turning to berth at the pier. A steamer has just departed. possibly heading for Glasgow.

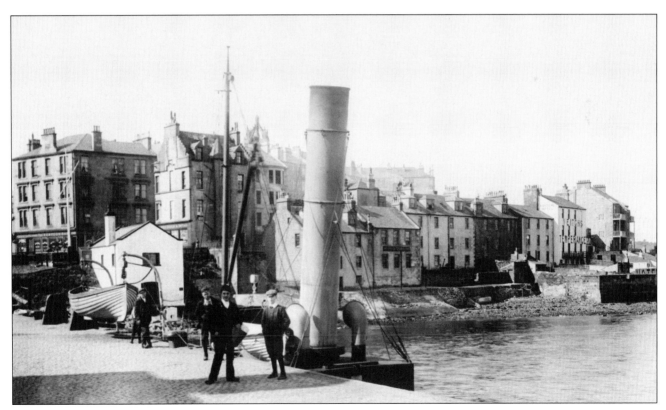

GOUROCK FROM THE PIER, SHOWING THE BACKS OF BUILDINGS ALONG KEMPOCK STREET,1900.   45975

Kempock Place is just in view on the extreme left of the picture. Over to the right is Seaton's temperance hotel, one of several in the town. At this time, temperance hotels abounded throughout the UK, but there was in fact little difference between them and private hotels because neither had liquor licences.

KEMPOCK STREET BETWEEN ALBERT ROAD AND SHORE STREET, GOUROCK, 1900. 45978

The total absence of road traffic, other than bicycles, and the fact that people appear to be in their best clothes, suggests that this picture was taken on a Sunday. Note the blinds on the shop windows and the attraction they hold for small boys.

THE ESPLANADE WITH THE PEBBLE BEACH IN EVIDENCE, 1900.
45969

As well as being a resort, Gourock was known for its herring curing. In 1688, the first recorded curing of red herrings took place here.

GLASGOW ROAD, CLYDEBANK, 1900.   C208004

On the left is the Clydebank Co-operative, a teetotal organisation which banned its members from selling alcohol until 1959.

CONGESTION ON THE NARROW BRIDGE IN KILBOWIE ROAD, 1900.   C208002

In 1881, the population of Clydebank was 1,600 people, most of which depended upon the shipyard. In 1882, the American firm of Singers opened a sewing-machine factory, bringing yet more jobs and more people to the area. Clydebank became a burgh in 1886.

GLASGOW ROAD, CLYDEBANK.
It's all eyes on the cameraman for this picture. Electric trams first ran in Glasgow in 1898 on the Mitchell Street to Springburn route. By 1909, there were about 95 miles of double-track tramway, including lines to Govan, Partick, Pollockshaws and Rutherglen.

C208005

DUMBARTON CASTLE, 1897.   39809

It was from here, in 1548, that six-year-old Mary, Queen of Scots left for France to marry the Dauphin when both were old enough. In return France offered Scotland military assistance against England.

HELENSBURGH ESPLANADE, 1901.   47402

In the distance and slightly to the left of the clock tower is the obelisk erected to the memory of Henry Bell, who built the first steam-powered vessel to sail on the Clyde. Another famous son of the town was J Logie Baird, the inventor of television.

COLQUHOUN SQUARE, HELENBURGH, 1901. 47405

Helensburgh's leading hotels were the Queen's and the Imperial. During the main season, rooms cost from 3s 6d a day and dinner was 4s, which was slightly less than the top Glasgow hotels charged.

PRINCES STREET, HELENBURGH, 1901. 47404

Helensburgh was described as 'a favourite watering place situated at the mouth of the Gareloch, laid out with the mathematical regularity of an American city'.

THE PIER AT TARBET, LOCH LOMOND, 1899.
Tarbet lies at the eastern end of a narrow neck of land that extends from Arrochar on Loch Long. In 1263, Magnus of Norway dragged his longships over the neck to Tarbet, using the loch to extend his raids into the hinterland.

43209

A BUSY DUNOON PIER, 1904.   52620

One steamer has just departed and there are two others berthed alongside. The one on the right appears to belong to the North British Railway, whilst the one on the left has funnel colours associated with Capt. John Williams and could be the *Strathmore*. In any one year, Dunoon could expect to handle about 10,000 calls by steamers.

THE ARGYLL HOTEL, DUNOON, 1904.   52614

This was one of three hotels recommended to overseas visitors; the others were the Queen's and McColl's. It was also possible to hire apartments in Dunoon at about 15s a week during the main season.

ROTHESAY ESPLANADE ON A SUNNY AFTERNOON, 1897.   39837
Rothesay's main hotels at this time were the Royal, the Queen's, and the Bute Arms. The Esplanade Hotel offered tea, bed and breakfast for 8s 6d per night.

THE GLENBURN HYDROPATHIC, 1899.   43210
A week's stay cost around 59s, although guests were not obliged to take any of the water treatments offered, but they were expected to refrain from drinking alcohol and had to take their meals together at prescribed hours.

A BUSTLING SCENE AT ROTHESAY PIER, 1897.
During the season, Rothesay's population of about 9,000 would increase dramatically.

39836

A HORSE-TRAM FROM PORT BANNATYNE MAKES ITS WAY ALONG ROTHESAY ESPLANADE. 39838
The tramway extended to Ettrick Bay on the west coast and was electrified in 1902.

THE MOATED RUINS OF ROTHESAY CASTLE, 1897. 39845
An earlier castle on the site was captured in 1263 by the Norse and was subsequently demolished, allegedly on the orders of Robert the Bruce. A new, stronger fortress was then built in its place.

TARBERT AT THE HEAD OF EAST LOCH TARBERT, AN INLET OF LOCH FYNE.   T102001
West Loch Tarbert is only a couple of miles away and it is said that in 1093 Magnus Barefoot dragged his longship overland between the two lochs, claiming Kintyre as a Norse possession.

NEAR THE NORTHERN TIP OF ARRAN, 1890.   A93001
A ruined fourteenth century double-towered castle stands guard over Lochranza. It was here that Robert Bruce is said to have landed on his return from Ireland in 1306.

MILLPORT, 1897.   39857

The Collegiate Church built in 1851 was consecrated the Episcopal Cathedral of Argyll and the Isles in 1876. Famous for the quality of its beaches, Millport developed as a resort following the construction of the harbour and the introduction of a ferry service to and from Largs. As late as the 1940s, there was only one bus, a few motor taxis and some horse-drawn cabs on the island.

A VIEW OF LARGS, 1897.   39851

Largs sheltered by the nearby island of Cumbrae, Largs has long been a popular place for messing about in boats. It was also a good centre for excursions by steamer to the Kyles of Bute, Loch Fyne and the Kilbrennan Sound.

SEVENTEENTH CENTURY PARISH CHURCH OF ST COLUMBA, 1897.   39855

This church in Largs is famous for the Skelmorlie Aisle, which contains the tombs of Sir Robert Montgomery and his wife. Another famous monument, the round tower at Bowen Craig commemorated the defeat of the Norsemen in 1263.

A CLOSER LOOK AT THE CHURCH AND SEAFRONT AT LARGS, 1897.   39856

Largs was well served by steamers from all parts of the Clyde, and by the Glasgow & South Western Railway to Ardrossan via Fairlie and West Kilbride. One of Largs's own well-travelled sons was Sir Thomas Brisbane, who became governor of New South Wales and had an Australian city named after him.

EGLINTON CASTLE, IRVINE, 1904.   53151

Standing between Kilwinning and Irvine the castle became famous in 1839 as the venue for a medieval tournament. Though not the first tournament to be held in Europe during the nineteenth century, it was the first and last to be held in the UK during the Gothic revival. In full armour, knights rode down the lists, trying to unhorse one another with lances.

THE HARBOUR AT IRVINE, 1904.   53154

The novelist John Galt was born in the town in 1779 but Irvine is more famous as the place where Robert Burns eked out a living as a flax-dresser between 1781 and 1783.

THE BRIG OF AYR, 1900. 46000

The 'Twa Brigs of Ayr' became famous thanks to a poem by Robert Burns. Things had changed by the time this photograph was taken. The Auld Brig which is thought to date from the thirteenth century, is still standing. The New Brig, was rebuilt in 1879 having lasted less than 100 years.

SANDGATE STREET LOOKING TOWARDS THE NEW BRIG AND BEYOND TO MAIN STREET, 1900. 46003

On the right, at the junction with High Street, are the town buildings, the handsome spire of which is considered to be one of the finest in the Lowlands.

WALLACE TOWER IN THE HIGH STREET, AYR, 1900.
The 130 ft high neo-Gothic building was completed in 1832. It replaced an earlier structure in which Sir William Wallace was alleged to have been imprisoned.

46002

THE BIRTHPLACE OF WILLIAM BURNS, ALLOWAY, 1897.   39858
Robert Burns was born here on the 25 January 1759. The cottage was rebuilt by the poet's father and later became an inn. In 1881 it was purchased by the trustees of the Burns Monument and opened as a museum.

THE ROOFLESS AND ALLEGEDLY HAUNTED KIRK AT ALLOWAY, 1897.   39861
Burns's father is buried in the churchyard.

CHAPTER 3
HIGHLANDS & ISLANDS

✆ KYLEAKIN ✆

At Kyleakin on the Isle of Skye stand the ruins of Castle Moil. It is said that the castle was built by the daughter of one of the Norse kings of the Western Isles. Legend has it that she had a boom placed across the narrow strait and any ship plying between Skye and the mainland had to pay a toll. In the 1990s tolls were once again the order of the day when the controversial Skye Road Bridge was opened.

✆ GLENFINNAN ✆

Prince Charles Edward Stuart landed at Eriksay off South Uist, MacDonald of Boisdale told him to go home. The prince left for the mainland, establishing a base near Arisaig, but here too Cameron of Lochiel also suggested that it would be best for all if the prince returned to Scotland. Not to be put off, Charles sailed on to Glenfinnan, landing on 19 August 1745.

✆ STAFFA ✆

Lying to the north-east of Iona, the uninhabited island of Staffa is famous for its caves and rock formations.

✆ IONA ✆

Only three miles long, Iona lies just off the extreme south-west of Mull. It was chosen by St Columba in AD 563 as the site for a religious house from where he could carry out his missionary work among the heathen.

✆ OBAN ✆

The town of Oban is only a little more than 200 years old. It owes its origins to the establishing of a fishing station by the government Fishery Board in 1786. The aim had been to develop commercial fishing in the Firth of Lorne. The project was eventually abandoned, but by this time Oban had begun to develop, albeit very slowly. Fishing and agriculture played an important part in the economy of the area, but it was the opening up of the Western Highlands to tourism that gave the town the boost it so desperately needed.

✆ INVERARY ✆

Inverary Castle, the eighteenth century home of the Dukes of Argyll, was designed by Roger Morris and Robert Mylne and completed in about 1780. During his visit to the Highlands, Dr Johnson was entertained here by the 5th Duke.

✆ FORTROSE ✆

Fortrose stands on the Black Isle overlooking the Inner Moray. The ruined cathedral dates from the reign of David I. Some of the stone was carted off by Cromwell's forces for use in the construction of a fort at Inverness.

∞ INVERNESS ∞

The area in and around Inverness has been occupied since ancient times and it was here, in the sixth century, that the capital of the Pictish kingdom stood. It is thought that Macbeth may have lived at Inverness Castle or used it as a base for operations against the Orcadians. Inverness will always be associated with Prince Charles Edward Stuart and the castle of Culloden Moor. Following the battle, 300 clansmen were herded into Inverness town jail and left without food or water for two days. With the jail bursting at the seams, churches, cellars and ships in the harbour were commandeered as prisons. All prisoners were stripped of their clothes and the wounded left unattended. Those that died were thrown into unmarked trenches.

∞ CAWDOR ∞

A few miles to the south of Nairn stands Cawdor Castle, one of Scotland's finest medieval buildings. It is of course famous for its association with Macbeth and the murder of Duncan.

GLENFINNAN AT THE HEAD OF LOCH SHIEL.   L135001

Here, with a few loyal retainers, Prince Charles waited for the clans. After three hours only 150 men of the clan Ranald had joined him. Then Cameron of Lochiel turned up with about 700 clansmen, followed by the MacDonalds of Keppoch. The royal standard was raised, and the fight to regain the throne for the house of Stuart was on. The monument was erected in 1815 by MacDonald of Glenaladale.

KYLEAKIN ON THE ISLE OF SKYE, c.1890.
The town overlooks the narrow strait of Kyle Akin, which is said to take its name from King Haakon who sailed this way on his way to Largs in 1263.

THE WILD AND ROCKY SCENERY OF GLEN TORRIDON, 1890.
The quartzite peaks of *Beinn Eighe* in the background. The UK's first National Nature Reserve was some miles away on the slopes of *Sgurr Ban*.

G80001

THE RUINS OF INVERLOCHY CASTLE, *c.*1890.

It was here in February 1645 that the troops of the after a forced march across difficult terrain in appaling weather, that the Marquis of Montrose defeated a 5,000 strong force of Campbells and Lowlanders. The clan power of Argyll is said to have been destroyed for a generation.

GLENCOE, 1890.

It was here, at dawn on 13 February 1692, that soldiers commanded by Campbell of Glen Lyon killed at least 40 out of the 200 MacDonalds living in the glen. Among the dead was the MacDonald chieftain MacIan of Glencoe who was buried on the island of Eilean Munde.

GLENCOE, 1899.

The reason for the Glencoe massacre was the failure of MacIan to swear allegiance to William III before 1 January 1692. MacIan had arrived at Fort William on 31 December, but was redirected to Inveraray with the result that he did not take the oath until 6 January.

DUART CASTLE ON THE ISLE OF MULL, 1903.

This is the ancestral home of the chiefs of the Macleans. The Macleans paid the price for siding with James VII against William III, forfeiting castle and estates. Duart was then garrisoned until the end of the eighteenth century when it was allowed to fall into ruin. Purchased back by Sir Fitzroy Maclean, Duart has been completely restored.

CORPACH ON THE NORTHERN SHORE OF LOCH EIL, 1890.
In the background to the south-east is Ben Nevis. The mountain once boasted a hostel and an observatory on its summit. The observatory lasted from 1883 to 1904, the hostel closed in 1915.

B267001

THIS IS FINGAL'S CAVE, 1903.   50897
The Legend has it that the cave was formed when the giant Finn McCoul made the island. Finn is also said to
have built the giant's causeway in Northern Ireland.

IONA, CATHEDRAL, 1903.   50889
St Columba was a member of the powerful O'Neill clan and left Ireland after the battle of *Cuil-dremne* in
which 3,000 men are thought to have died. It is said that it was Columba himself who caused the battle,
accused by the High King of taking a psalter without permission. Columba appealed to his clan for help in
clearing his name, and the matter was settled by sword and axe.

THE RUINED ROMANESQUE ST ORAN'S CHAPEL, 1903. 50892
Iona is the oldest Christian burial ground in Scotland and contains the graves of many kings and chieftains.
Among those buried here are Kenneth MacAlpine, the first Celtic king of Scotland, and Duncan, who was
murdered by Macbeth in 1040.

A VIEW OF IONA, 1903. 50887
In 1203, the Benedictines founded a monastery on Iona which lasted until the Reformation. In 1899, the 8th
Duke of Argyll presented the ruins of the abbey to the Church of Scotland in the hope that restoration work
might be undertaken. The building was eventually re-roofed, and used for worship once again in 1910.

THE DOG STONE OR *Clach a Choin*, 1901. 47513

The legendary Fingal is said to have tied his dog Bran to the stone. In the distance is the ruined McDougall fortress of Dunollie Castle, which overlooks the Firth of Lorne.

GEORGE STREET, OBAN, 1901. 47511

On the right is the Caledonian Hotel, one of a number of hotels in the town. The Great Western and the Alexandria were the most expensive, and the Marine was well spoken of. There were three temperance hotels, one of which can be seen next to the King's Arms.

THE SOUND OF KERRERA, 1903.   50885

The Island of Kerrera faces Oban and is linked to the town by a ferry service. On the island is the ruined Gylen Castle where king Alexander II died of fever in 1249. There is also a memorial to David Hutcheson, the pioneer of steamboat services to the Western Isles.

LOOKING ACROSS THE SWEEP OF OBAN BAY, 1900.   O4001

The railway station is in the foreground with the north pier and esplanade on the far side of the bay beyond the yachts and steamers.

INVERARAY, *c.*1890.
Time for a paddle at Inveraray.

I15003

INVERARY, 1899.

The town was originally closer to the old castle but was relocated in the mid eighteenth century. It was to Inverary that MacIan of Glencoe was sent to swear allegiance to William III. MacIan's unavoidable delay in reaching Inverary led to the massacre of Glencoe.

FORTROSE, 1880.

Fortrose was originally called Chanonry. It was made a royal burgh in 1592. In January of that year a hoard of silver coins dating from the time of Robert III were unearthed near the ruins of the cathedral.

THE CROMARTY FIRTH TOWN OF DINGWALL, 1890.   D77001

This was the home town of General Hector MacDonald (1853-1903), who enlisted in the 92nd Highlanders at the age of 17. In 1879, MacDonald distinguished himself during the First Afghan War, and General Roberts offered him a Victoria Cross or a commission. He chose the commission saying that he would win the Victoria Cross later.

WASH-DAY AT ONE OF THE STRATHPEFFER HOTELS, c.1890.   S241003

The village was a popular spa having both sulphur and chalybeate springs. It was served by a branch line of the Highland Railway from Fodderty Junction.

THE VIEW FROM INVERNESS CASTLE, 1890.   I255003

The suspension bridge superseded a stone bridge of seven arches which was destroyed during severe flooding in 1849. The suspension bridge itself lasted until 1961 when it was demolished.

THE BATTLEFIELD OF CULLODEN MOOR, 1890.   I255001

On the right is the memorial cairn built in 1881 by Arthur Forbes of Culloden and the headstones erected over the graves of the clans.

CAWDOR CASTLE, *c.*1890.

The keep dates from 1454 and some parts are thought to be even older. The castle was extensively altered during the sixteenth and seventeenth centuries and again in the nineteenth.

C21200I

CULLODEN HOUSE, 1903.
The house stands two miles north-west of the battlefield. In 1746 it was the home of Duncan Forbes, Lord President of the Court of Session. It was later burnt down and was rebuilt between 1772 and 1783.

I255002

CHAPTER 4
GRAMPIAN

⤳ Braemar ⤲

The village of Braemar is situated on the banks of Cluny Burn. It was here, in 1715, that a number of Scottish lords, including the Earl of Mar, met on the pretext of a hunting trip to plan an uprising against the House of Hanover and return the Stuarts to the throne of Scotland.

⤳ Fraserburgh ⤲

Fraserburgh was founded in the sixteenth century, as Farthlie, in a charter granted to the 7th Laird of Philorth Alexander Fraser. In 1595, a university was founded thanks to a grant from the Scottish parliament. Unfortunately, this seat of learning lasted only a decade or so due to its principal being arrested on the orders of James VI. The university never recovered and faded into obscurity.

⤳ Aberdeen ⤲

Now Scotland's third largest city, Aberdeen's charters date back to around 1179 although St Machar is said to have founded a church here in AD 580. These days, Aberdeen is famous for its association with North Sea oil but shipbuilding, fishing, papermaking and the quarrying of granite have all played their part in the city's development. Aberdeen's history contains one or two dark episodes. In 1336, both Old and New Aberdeen were burned down by Edward III. Then at the end of September 1644 on Black Friday the city suffered again. The Royalist Marquis of Montrose, a combined Highland and Irish force, sent an emissary and a young drummer-boy under a flag of truce to demand the town's surrender. Something went wrong and the drummer-boy was shot dead. In a bitter rage, Montrose promised his troops that they could sack the burgh once they had taken it. Despite putting up a strong resistance, Aberdeen fell and there then followed three nights of pillage, rape and plunder, in which about 200 citizens were slaughtered.

THE MILL ON THE CLUNY AT BRAEMAR, 1880.

Among the visitors to the village was Robert Louis Stevenson, while spending a winter here he wrote *Treasure Island*.

B266002

CAIRNWELL PASS, 1880. B266003
The road south from Braemar climbs through Glen Clunie and then over the rugged Cairnwell Pass.

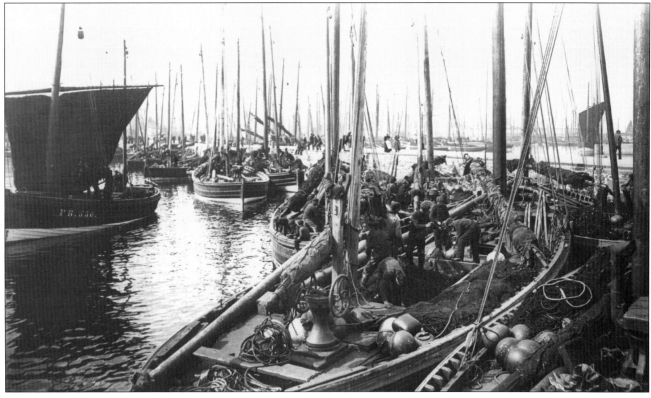

PART OF FRASERBURGH'S HERRING FLEET, 1900. F63002
Fishing was an important local industry and in 1914 there were more than 200 boats registered here.

THE AULD BRIG O' DON, OR BRIDGE OF BALGOWNIE, ABERDEEN, 1890.   A90004
The single-span bridge is situated a few hundred yards to the north of St Machar's Cathedral. It dates from the early fourteenth century.

LOOKING ALONG UNION STREET, ABERDEEN, c.1885.   A90005
On the right is the Mercat Cross dating from 1686. It was built at a cost of £100, paid for out of guild wine funds. Beyond the cross are the municipal buildings complete with 210 ft tower.

UNION STREET, WHEN ELECTRIC TRAMCARS FIRST RAN IN THE CITY, ABERDEEN, *c*.1899.
The chief thoroughfare of Aberdeen, Union Street at this time was three-quarters of a mile long, 70 ft wide and built entirely of granite.

A90009

QUEEN'S CORNER AND ST NICHOLAS STREET, ABERDEEN, *c.*1899.
There is some activity around the base of the statue and although identification is difficult it is possible that two ladies are selling flowers and/or button holes.

QUEEN'S CORNER

A90007

UNION TERRACE AND GARDENS, *c.*1899.   A90008

Nearby is the Grand Hotel (rooms 4*s* 6*d*, dinner 5*s*), the parish council building, the school board offices and a statue of Robert Burns.

THE RUINS OF DUNNATTOR CASTLE, *c.*1900.   D80401

The castle stood to the south of Stonehaven on a rocky headland overlooking the North Sea. It was here, in July 1650, that Charles II was entertained by the Earl Marischal. It was the only fortress in Scotland that flew the Stuart royal flag after Charles's defeat at Worcester in 1651. Dunnattor held out until May 1652, when Sir George Ogilvy of Barras was allowed to surrender with all the honours of war.

CHAPTER 5
TAYSIDE

✺ BRECHIN ✺

This small Tayside town once played host to one of the significant events in Scotland's history. John Balliol surrendered the realm of Scotland to Edward Longshanks here on 10 July 1296. When Balliol walked into the hall of Brechin Castle to meet Bishop Anthony Bek of Durham, the Bishop ripped the red and gold arms of Scotland off Balliol's tunic. Balliol was known afterwards as Toom Tabard.

✺ PERTH ✺

An ancient royal burgh, Perth was once capital of Scotland. It was at Perth, in 1559, that John Knox gave his famous sermon from the pulpit of St John's Church. Knox delivered such a powerful and emotive speech against idolatry that it is regarded by many as the start of the Reformation in Scotland.

DAVID STREET, BRECHIN, 1900.   B275002

The Frith cameraman found himself with an audience when he took this picture. Brechin's famous landmark at this time was the Round Tower, dating from the tenth or eleventh centurys and one of only two examples of round towers in Scotland.

A VIEW OVER MONCRIEFFE ISLAND AND THE TAY, PERTH, 1901.
Cutting across the middle of the picture is the bridge carrying the Caledonian Railway, while on the far right is the Victoria Road bridge. Between the two are the county buildings, which occupy the site of the house in which the Gowrie conspiracy against James VI was hatched in 1600.

47430

THE POST OFFICE AND NEW SCOTT STREET, PERTH, 1899. 43901

Among documents preserved locally is a letter written by John Blair dated 7 November 1689. Blair was the postmaster-general and in the letter he details the establishment of a postal service in the city.

HIGH STREET EAST, PERTH, 1899. 43899

By this time the population of Perth was about 32,000. The city's manufacturing industries were pretty diverse and included linen, twine, jute, glassmaking and printing.

PERTH BRIDGE AND MONUMENT, 1899.   43897

Built of rose-red sandstone, Perth Bridge was completed in 1771. The city then had a population of nearly 8,000. It was still an important port with several hundred vessels coming up river every year to discharge and take on cargo.

THE VILLAGE OF SCONE, 1897.   43917

Scone was where Scotland's kings were crowned. On 1 January 1651, Charles II was crowned King of Scotland with Robert the Bruce's gold circlet. His coronation was bought at a price. Charles agreed to impose the Presbyterian Church in England and the third civil war was about to begin.

COMRIE STREET, CRIEFF, 1904.
Crieff was originally called Drummond. In January 1716, the place was totally destroyed when the Jacobites put the town to the torch. It was rebuilt thanks to the efforts of James Drummond, 3rd Duke of Perth.

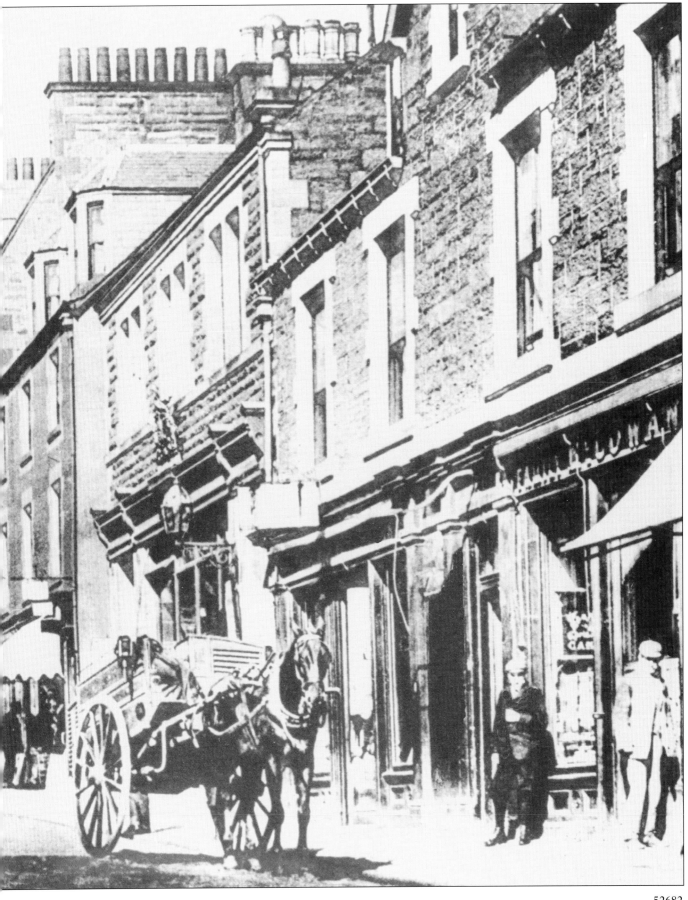

52682

THIS IS THE HIGH STREET, CRIEFF, 1899. 43926

On his retreat north in 1745, Prince Charles Edward Stuart held a council of war in Crieff at the Drummond Arms.

COMRIE FROM THE EAST, 1899. 44405

Situated between Crieff and St Fillans on the Highland fault line, Comrie is famous for the number of earth tremors experienced by its inhabitants. due to the village lying on the Highland fault line. The first recorded tremor was in 1789, and the most sustained were a series of 20 within 24 hours, one day in 1839.

CHAPTER 6
CENTRAL SCOTLAND & FIFE

ᘒ STIRLING ᘒ

Stirling is the last place where there is a bridge over the Forth before the river widens into an estuary. The town and its castle have therefore been fought over on numerous occasions. In 1297 the castle was captured by William Wallace but retaken by Longshanks in 1304 after a siege lasting three months. Ten years later it fell to the Bruce after the Battle of Bannockburn. Following their defeat at the Battle of Dunbar on 3 September 1650, Major General David Leslie and several thousand survivors of his army, took shelter in Stirling. After pursuing Leslie from Dunbar, Oliver Cromwell decided not to attempt a siege of Stirling Castle and withdrew to Edinburgh. Stirling eventually fell to General Monck.

ᘒ ABERDOUR, FIFE ᘒ

Aberdourm, lying between Burntisland and Dalgety Bay, is described in the 1906 Baedeker as 'a favourite little sea-bathing place, with an old castle and the ruins of a Norman church'.

AN OLD MILL ON THE RIVER DOCHART AT KILLIN, 1890.   K51004

Not far away is the ruined Breadalbane stronghold of Finlarig Castle. One of its more interesting features is what is thought to be an ancient beheading pit.

AN EXCURSION STEAMER AT LOCH KATRINE PIER, *c.*1890.

The Loch, which is ringed with hills, features in Sir Walter Scott's poem *The Lady of the Lake.*

LOCH ACHRAY, *c.*1899. 44603

This Loch is sandwiched between Loch Katrine and Loch Vennachar. This small, perfectly formed Loch Achray. This picture was taken in 1899 shows the Trossachs Hotel situated on the northern shore and the wooded slopes of *Sron Armailte* behind.

THE BRIDGE AND CATHEDRAL OF DUNBLANE, 1899. 44651

The body of the cathedral dates from the thirteenth century; the tower is Norman. During the sixteenth century, the roof of the nave collapsed and was not finally restored until 1893.

STIRLING CASTLE, 1899.

One of Scotland's greatest royal fortresses, Stirling Castle was taken by William Wallace in 1297 but was surrendered to Edward I in August 1305 following a siege. The survivors of the garrison, commanded by Sir William Oliphant, were brought before Longshanks and made to kneel in supplication.

44696

Bridge of Allan, 1899.

44675

Robert Louis Stevenson was a frequent visitor to Allan when the town was a popular Victorian spa complete with pump room and baths.

Stirling Castle, 1899.

44697

It was here at Stirling Castle that both James II and James V were born and where Mary, Queen of Scots and James VI both lived for a number of years. The Parliament Hall is close to the Inner Court and James VI's Chapel Royal.

STIRLING BRIDGE, 1899. 44701

Dating from about 1400, the bridge was for many years one of only a handful of crossing points over the Forth. In 1745, one of the arches was blown up to prevent Prince Charles Edward's forces from entering the town.

BROAD STREET LOOKING TOWARDS THE UNCOMPLETED MAR'S WARK, STIRLING, 1899. 44705

Dating from 1570, the uncompleted renaissance building was intended for use by the Earl of Mar who was Regent.

An excursion steamer from Leith about to depart from the stone pier, Aberdour, 1900. The steamer is going astern to clear Silverlands Bay, before turning and heading back across the Forth.

45912

CHAPTER 7

LOTHIAN

⬧ EDINBURGH ⬧

The capital of Scotland. The Old Town as it was called grew eastward along the ridge from the castle down to where Holyroodhouse would eventually be built. Much of the Old Town was rebuilt in the middle of the sixteenth century following a major fire, but even then it remained notoriously cramped and insanitary. The only way for the inhabitants to get rid of their refuse and empty their chamber pots was by throwing the stuff into the street at night. Thankfully, there were refuse men who came in the wee small hours to shovel it up and cart it away. On Dr Johnson's first visit to Edinburgh in August 1773, he is said to have met Boswell in the High Street with the words, 'Sir I smell you in the dark.' The New Town dates from 1768 and is centred on the three parallel thoroughfares of Princes Street, George Street and Charlotte Street.

⬧ NEWHAVEN ⬧

A little more than one mile to the west of Leith is the small fishing village of Newhaven. It was here that James IV founded a royal dockyard where he could build his navy. The first ship that was launched was the *Great Michael,* a huge warship by the standards of the day, capable of carrying 420 gunners and 1,000 soldiers.

⬧ NORTH BERWICK ⬧

In 1591 some women were accused of being witches and receiving the Devil in St Andrew's Church. At their subsequent trial, the women confessed that they knew the secrets of the king's bedchamber and that their satanic leader was none other than Francis Stewart, Earl of Bothwell. The king, who believed in witchcraft, ordered Bothwell's arrest. Bothwell escaped but came back at Christmas and attacked Holyroodhouse. The king's advisers, who also believed in witchcraft, considered Bothwell's appearance to be a divine warning. Bothwell was driven off but came back demanding a trial, which was not granted. Bothwell left Scotland and died in poverty in Naples.

THE RUINS OF LINLITHGOW PALACE, 1897.   39154
Situated upon the south shore of Linlithgow Loch, It was in this Palace, in 1542, that Mary, Queen of Scots
was born. Situated upon the south shore of Linlithgow Loch, the palace is thought to have been burnt down
accidently in 1746 by General Hawley's troops.

LOTHIAN, 1897.   39157
All is peace and quiet in this scene, but things were livelier on 23 January 1570. Lord James Stewart, Earl of
Moray and Regent, was shot by James Hamilton as he rode through the town. The assassin fired his musket
from an upper window in a house belonging to the archbishop of St Andrews, who also appears to have
supplied the getaway horse. The archbishop was executed at Stirling in 1571 without the formality of a trial.

HOLYROOD HOUSE.   39168

Work on the palace began during the reign of James IV and continued under James V. On the left are the remains of the Chapel Royal, which is in fact the nave of an abbey founded in 1128.

THE CANONGATE TOLBOOTH, 1897.   39124A

Note the poles used for drying washing. When this picture was taken, the tolbooth was already more than 300 years old, having been built at the end of the sixteenth century. It has had a varied career, having been used as a courthouse and a prison.

THE GRASSMARKET, 1883.

The site of many an execution and the location of the Porteous Riots in 1736. John Porteous was appointed captain of one of the companies employed to keep the peace. He soon gained a reputation for exceeding his authority. At a riot following the execution of a man named Robertson, Porteous ordered his men to fire on the crowd. He was later taken into custody, tried and condemned to death but a stay of execution was

granted until the king returned from Hanover. On 7 September, a mob broke into the jail took Porteous to the Grassmarket and lynched him. Despite a large reward being offered for information, no one was ever charged with killing Porteous.

EDINBURGH CASTLE FROM JOHNSTON TERRACE, 1897. 39120

Though he managed to occupy the city in 1745, Prince Charles Edward Stuart failed to capture its fortress.

THE SCOTT MONUMENT, 1900. E24510

The monument was designed by George Kemp and completed in 1844. During his lifetime Scott lived at several addresses in the city, the most famous being 39 Castle Street, where he wrote many of the Waverley novels.

A VIEW ACROSS WAVERLEY BRIDGE, 1883.   E24302
Cockburn Street twists and climbs up to the High Street. On the right, the famous crown spire of St Giles's
Church can be seen above the rooftops.

PRINCES STREET, 1897.   39108
Prince's Street looking west.

PRINCE'S STREET WEST END, EDINBURGH, 1897.   39113
This was fashionable place to shop and eat out with several highly recommended restaurants including Ferguson & Forrester, Littlejohns and the Royal British. Leading confectioners were Mackies and Ritchies where shortbread was a speciality.

THE JUNCTION OF HOPE STREET, QUEENSFERRY STREET & SANDWICK STREET, EDINBURGH, 1887.39114
St John's and St Cuthbert's churches provide the backdrop along with the castle .

THE CASTLE FROM PRINCE'S GARDENS, EDINBURGH, 1897.   39119
The gardens and the railway occupy what was Nor' Loch, an expanse of water that formed part of the old city's defences. It was drained at the same time as nearby marshland in the late eighteenth century to allow Edinburgh to grow.

NEWHAVEN, 1897.   39139
One Sunday in May 450 years earlier, the people woke to find an English invasion fleet off shore. Henry VIII's troops had come to collect debts owed by the Scots because of their violation of two treaties signed at Greenwich in July 1543.

THE FORTH BRIDGE, 1897.
Built between 1883 and 1890 the bridge was constructed to carry the North British Railway's main line between Edinburgh and Aberdeen. It has an overall length of 2,700 yards including approach viaducts. The tracks run across the bridge 150 ft above sea level.

39145

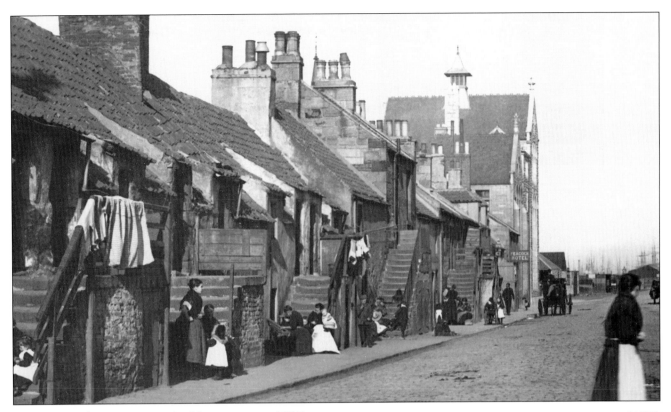

FISHERMEN'S COTTAGES AT NEWHAVEN, 1897.   39137
The fishermen's wives were noted for their dresses which probably reflected their Dutch and Scandinavian origins. They were also known for their cries when selling fish; 'Caller Herrin' (fresh herrings) and 'Caller Ou' (fresh oysters).

A VIEW DOWN QUALITY STREET, NORTH BERWICK, 1897.   39176
The opening of the railway branch line put North Berwick within easy reach of Edinburgh making it a popular place for people working in Edinburgh to live, no less than 58,000 passengers travelled by train from North Berwick, the majority to Edinburgh.

THE MARINE HOTEL AND THE GOLF LINKS, 1897.   39177

By the beginning of the twentieth century, North Berwick was beginning to rival St Andrews. Prices for rooms and meals at the Marine and the Royal hotels were on a par with the top hotels in central Glasgow and Edinburgh.

THE SUBSTANTIAL RUINS OF THE DOUGLAS STRONGHOLD OF TANTALLON CASTLE, 1897.   39186

This fortress, with its distinctive rose-red brickwork, was destroyed by General Monck's troops in 1651.

Chapter 8
THE BORDERS

∽ HAWICK ∽

In 1771, a local magistrate brought the first stocking-frames to Hawick. This was the start of the town's successful knitwear, woollen, yarn and hosiery manufacturing. Two hundred years later, there were 20 firms employing more than 5,000 workers.

THE HORSE MONUMENT, *c.*1955.   H248002

In 1514, an English raiding party were defeated at Hornshole Bridge by the young men of Hawick, many of the older men having been killed at the Battle of Flodden. The Horse Monument is a memorial to the victory.

THE JIMMIE GUTHRIE MONUMENT, HAWICK, *c.*1955.

The motorcycle racing star Jimmie Guthrie who was tragically killed in Germany in 1937.

TITLES AVAILABLE NOW

COUNTY SERIES

Berkshire, Buckinghamshire, Derbyshire, Greater London, Kent, Lake District, Lancashire, Leicestershire, London, Norfolk, Sussex, West Yorkshire and Yorkshire

TOWN & CITY SERIES

Brighton & Hove, Canterbury, Edinburgh, Glasgow & Clydeside, Norwich and York

COUNTRY SERIES

Ireland, North Wales, Scotland and South Wales

POSTER BOOKS

Canals and Waterways, Derbyshire, High Days and Holidays, Kent, Lake District, London, Railways, Canterbury and Derby

TITLES AVAILABLE FROM MARCH TO JULY 1999

COUNTY SERIES

Warwickshire, Staffordshire, Devon, Cheshire, Nottinghamshire, Cornwall, Surrey, Hampshire, Highlands, Hertfordshire, North Yorkshire and Wiltshire

TOWN & CITY SERIES

Maidstone, Bradford, Colchester, Dublin, Leeds, Buxton, Bristol, Nottingham, Manchester, Matlock, Macclesfield, St Ives, Derby, Sevenoaks, Newbury, Bognor Regis, Leicester, East Grinstead, Newark, Sheffield, Cambridge, Penzance, Eastbourne, Llandudno, Torquay, Whitby, Scarborough, Faversham to Herne Bay, Scilly Isles, Dorset Coast, Falmouth, Newquay, Bakewell, Lincoln, Barnstaple, Great Yarmouth, Blackpool and Dartmoor

IF YOU WOULD LIKE MORE INFORMATION PLEASE CONTACT:
WATERTON PRESS, WATERTON INDUSTRIAL ESTATE,
BRIDGEND, GLAMORGAN, CF31 3XP.
TEL: 01656 668836   FAX: 01656 668710

Half-Price VOUCHER

This voucher entitles you to a
Half Price Framed or Mounted print

All prints are A4 sepia, mounted in a cream mount with bevel cut aperture and single burgundy ruled line. Frames are dark polished wood and supplied ready to hang. Overall size approx 15 x 12in.

SPECIAL OFFER PRICES

Framed Print £16.45 (normally £32.90)
Mounted Print £9.97 (normally £19.95)

Simply select any photograph in this book that you would like to receive as a framed or mounted print, and complete the form below.

Page & Negative Number	Town & Description

I enclose a cheque/postal order for £...............
which includes p&p, made payable to
"The Francis Frith Collection."
OR Please debit my Mastercard/Visa

Number...

Expires.................Signature.............................

Mr/Mrs/Miss/Ms

Initial...................Surname...............................

Address...

....

Town...

County...

Postcode ....

Daytime Telephone No. (in case of queries)

....

Send your voucher and remittance to:
The Francis Frith Collection
Dept FF018, Frith's Barn, Teffont,
Salisbury, Wilts, SP3 5QP.
Fax: 01722 716 881